We Need Air to Breathe

Jill Andersen

Rosen REAL READERS

Rosen Classroom™
New York

People need air to breathe.

Air helps people live.

Plants are important.

Plants make air.

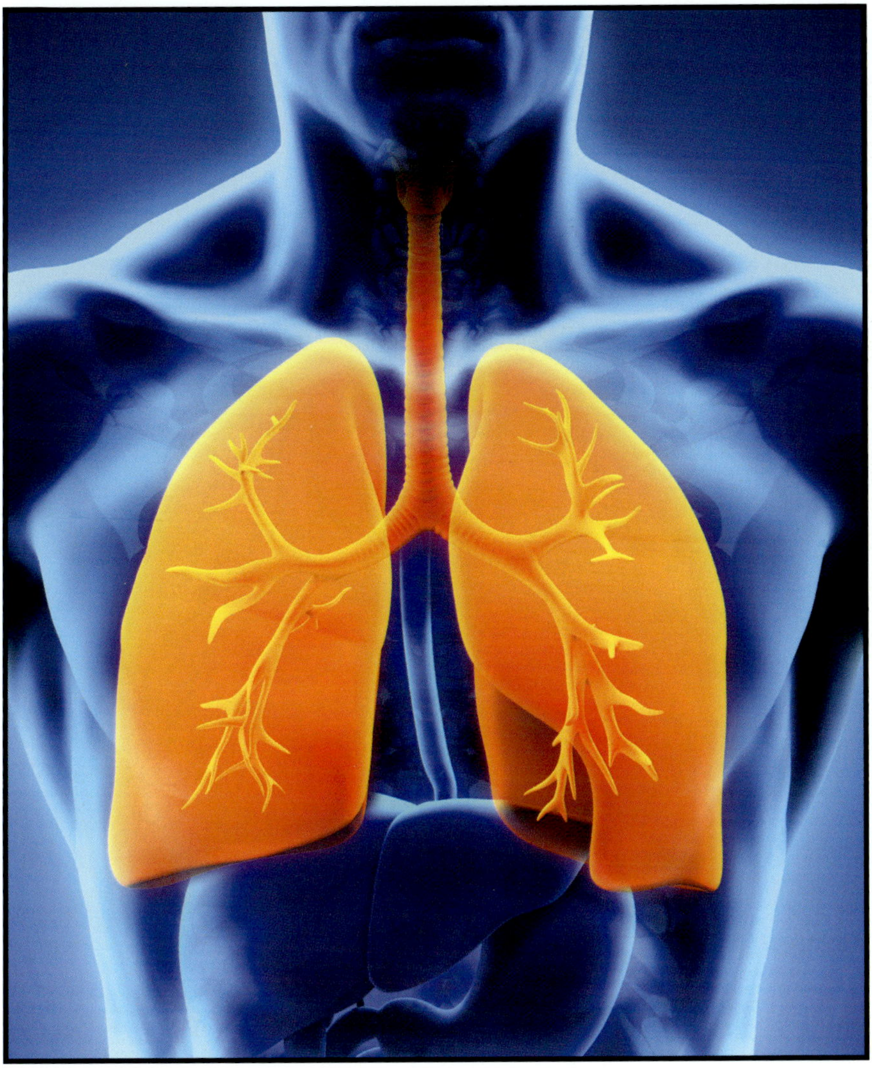

People breathe air
into their lungs.

People cannot breathe
underwater.
They use special tanks.

People cannot breathe
in space.
They use special tanks, too.

Words to Know

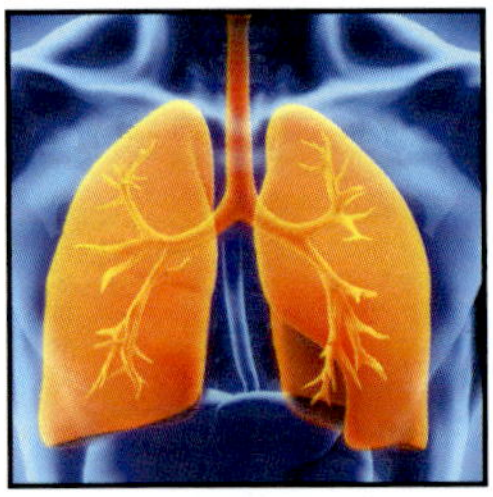

lungs

plants

space

underwater